THE
FREEDOM
PROTECTION PLAN

For PERMANENT Financial Safety
In Financially Unsafe Times

By: Tim Whipple

Copyright © 2024
All rights reserved.
ISBN-979-8-9915448-0-1

Also by Wealth Express®

HOW TO HAVE FINANCIAL CERTAINTY
IN UNCERTAIN ECONOMIC TIMES
(EVEN IF A CRASH COMES)

Wall Street Is NOT Your Friend - Watch Out!
Don't Outlive Your Money!

To learn more, please visit:
https://wealthexpress.ai/bp-protection-plan/

TABLE OF CONTENTS

INTRODUCTION 9
Please Read Every Word Of This Book. 9
  Why Is This Essential Reading? 9
You Can't Know What's Going 10
To Happen Next 10
  IMAGINE BEING ABLE TO 11
  QUICKLY AND EASILY... 11
Word On The Street Is This... 12
Warren Buffett's Secret 13
All Those Money-Hungry Vampire Ads 15
Can You Invest With A Plan 19
That Insures Your Way of Living? 19
  1. A Guaranteed Paycheck Every Month 20
  For The Rest Of Your Life 20
  2. It's Guaranteed Safe 20
  3. You Get Guaranteed Returns 21
  4. It Can Be A Great Way To Save On Taxes 21
  5. You Could Get A Really Big Bonus 23
  6. Not Portfolio Diversity — INCOME Diversity 23
  7. It Really Is Guaranteed? 24
  8. Guaranteed Income = Guaranteed Freedom 25
Is Guaranteed Income For Life For You? 26
  What To Do Next 26
What To Expect From Your Private, ... 27
At-Home Meeting 27
A Brief Personal Note 29

Who Benefits From Guaranteed Income For Life Plans? — 32

- Active, Lively Retirees — 33
- Single and Widowed Retirees — 34
- People Who Take Their Finances — 35
- And Retirement Seriously — 35
- And Take Responsibility For It. — 35
- The Retired or Soon-To-Be Retirees — 36
- With A Need For Income From Their — 36
- Life's Savings WITHOUT Undue Risk — 36
- Women Responsible For Their — 37
  - Own Finances Or Who May Become Responsible For Their Own Finances. — 37
- People With "Tax Bombs" — 38
- People Who Want To Enjoy Their Retirement Are A Perfect Fit For Wealth Express — 39
- Why You CAN'T Rely on Government — 40

SOCIAL SECURITY — 43

- WARNING: — 43

Gary + Judy — 45

- Do you take this personally? — 50
- You can STOP this anxiety. — 51
- WHY ARE WE NAMED — 52
- "WEALTH EXPRESS"? — 52
- I'LL BET — 54
- 3 Things You Need To Know… — 55
- Foundation First — 56

Margaret — 57

Is Your Retirement INSURED? 61
Did You Know?... 62
How Would You Like 63
A Retirement Income "Pay Raise"? 63
WHAT YOU MAY NOT KNOW & 64
PROBABLY HAVEN'T BEEN TOLD 64
A GUARANTEED INCOME FOR 66
LIFE PLAN CAN HELP 66
The Benefits of Delaying 70
Social Security Benefits 70

Ronald & Chester – 72
A Tale Of Two Retirements 72

Ronald: 73
The High-Flying Vice President 73
Chester: The Steady Foreman 74
    The Diverging Paths: Retirement Approaches 75
    The Retirement Years: 77
    A Tale of Two Futures 77
    YOUR SIX IMPORTANT QUESTIONS WILL BE ANSWERED AT YOUR FREE IN-HOME MEETING WITH A WEALTH EXPRESS® CERTIFIED ADVISOR 78
    Would You Rather... 79

WHAT IF?....
almost every source of information
about retirement investing has been
deliberately, massively confusing?
Making it so complicated you just
"surrender" and sign where they put
the sticky yellow Post-it notes?

WHAT IF?....
their advice, their
pie-charts, their market risk
portfolios FAIL TO "INSURE"
YOUR WAY OF LIVING, FOR LIFE?

INTRODUCTION

PLEASE READ EVERY WORD OF THIS BOOK.

It could make the very difference between struggling financially up to your very last breath... or living the comfortable, financially free retirement you've always dreamed of and intended.

WHY IS THIS ESSENTIAL READING?

Consider this: 40% of people *run out of money during retirement.* What most have in common is: they didn't think it could happen to them! And in most cases, it's not their fault. Despite their best efforts and intentions, instead of enjoying time with the grandkids, traveling, pursuing new interests, and simply relaxing…they're awake late at night wondering, worrying, and stressing about money. That's no way to live or retire. It is NOT necessary.

Why does this happen? Just look at all of the circumstances beyond your control that affect how far your retirement dollar actually goes. As of this writing, inflation is bleeding everyone dry. The stock market could collapse (again) at any time killing off your investments. The housing market can collapse (again), trouncing your 401k. Taxes shoot up. Social Security income plummets because someone in Washington decides to "tinker" with it. It's a constant battle.

YOU CAN'T KNOW WHAT'S GOING TO HAPPEN NEXT

But you can prepare for the worst financial storms. You can make informed decisions that protect your finances and your future. Guaranteed Income For Life means just that: Locking in income that PAYS YOU EACH MONTH. Just like when you used to receive a paycheck from your job or your own business.

Most retirement investing involves a myriad of risks AND IT'S NEVER DONE. You and/or your financial person/people are always actively managing, market-watching, adjusting, making new decisions. But you can actually BE DONE with all that. You can put your Freedom Protection Plan in place and "set it AND FORGET IT".

So read this book. Read every word. Size up this information for yourself. Decide if it's right for you, for your family. Guaranteed Income For Life is not for everyone. But it's perfect for anyone who prioritizes safety, security, and certainty when it comes to investing in retirement.

Sincerely,

Tim Whipple

Wealth Express® Ambassador

PS: As a pastor for many years, I sadly witnessed quite a few of our seniors unpleasantly surprised at quite literally running out of money, having to shrink their way of living. Others even forced into dignity-killing bankruptcy by huge medical bills or just a big stock market crash. Much of this was heartbreaking. That's why I accepted this position. And why I use this Plan and have shared this Plan with my family.

IMAGINE BEING ABLE TO QUICKLY AND EASILY...

- Lock in Guaranteed Income For Life with No Risk and No Loss of Principal
- DIVORCE THE IRS, paying as few taxes as legally possible in order to keep more of your savings
- Make your 401k and IRA "market-proof" so you never have to worry about the ups and downs of the market
- Get a "paycheck" EVERY MONTH just like you did before you retired.
- It isn't just possible...it's easy!

If that appeals to you, KEEP READING:

WORD ON THE STREET IS THIS...

Bankers can offer you Guaranteed Income For Life, with returns much higher than the painfully low returns you get with CDs and interest-bearing accounts. But they don't like to talk about it unless customers bring it up. And it is not their primary business or area of specialized knowledge.

Financial advisors can set you up with Guaranteed Income For Life. But they'd much rather you invest in the financial products that are more profitable to THEM. They prefer having you active in the stock, bond, muni-bond, ETF, etc markets requiring constant re-doing of your portfolio.

WARREN BUFFETT'S SECRET

Perhaps most incredible of all...
WARREN BUFFETT...

Word on the street has it that Warren Buffett invested in three separate Guaranteed Income For Life programs...BUT he does not list them on his investment reports.

Insiders believe the government is paying him to keep quiet about it.

Why? Because EVERYONE listens to Warren Buffett for investment advice. If he were to publicly praise Guaranteed Income For Life, EVERYONE would rush in. The government would lose a massive amount of tax revenue. Financial Advisor profits would plummet. And Wall Street would have a much harder time juking people out of their money. Shed no tears.

It doesn't matter how Guaranteed Income For Life affects their balance sheet. What's important is what it will do for you: provide increased monthly income from your savings and investments while strengthening the safety and security of your hard-earned money...and legally reducing the tax bite of your retirement income.

Guaranteed Income For Life gives you a paycheck each month.

No risk, no loss of principal. It has long-term growth potential. It's customizable based on your financial goals. Once locked in, your income cannot be reduced. (Ordinary company pensions CAN be.) Even if you live to be 105, your income continues and cannot be reduced.

A Guaranteed Income For Life "solid foundation" helps you prepare carefully for a stable retirement.

ALL THOSE MONEY-HUNGRY VAMPIRE ADS

HAVE YOU SEEN ALL THE ADS inviting you to "sell your life insurance policy for cash"? That happens at a big loss to you. It's a rather ghoulish business called "viatical settlements". They invest in your expected death. If you ever thought of life insurance as a way to protect your retirement, this tells you it fails. With some policies, you may be allowed to borrow a small amount from the insurance company. Or you can discount it and sell it to these vampires.

AND HAVE YOU SEEN ALL THE ADS FOR "REVERSE MORTGAGES"? These can be useful. But the fact that they are constantly advertised on TV every day and night tells you a lot of retired people are in tough financial straits and have no choice but to give up their homes. They get cash and to live in them, but when they die, the company owns their house—it can't be passed on to their families.

ALL THIS PROVES THAT BAD THINGS HAPPEN TO GOOD PEOPLE. ENTIRELY UNEXPECTED TRAGEDIES CAN VACUUM UP SOMEBODY'S RETIREMENT SAVINGS.

But none of this…nothing… can ever take away your Guaranteed Income For Life, locked in by The Freedom Protection Plan®!

Guaranteed Income For Life provides income for you to enjoy now AND allows you to pass on everything you worked for without sacrificing too much in taxes…all literally GUARANTEED.

Guaranteed Income For Life removes your worries and anxiety about outliving your money…and replaces them with CERTAINTY—in a very uncertain world.

Here is what Guaranteed Income For Life is NOT:
It's not a bright, flashy, high-risk, high-reward, swing-for-the-fences investment. If you're looking for get-rich-quick scenarios, this is not the product for you.

Guaranteed Income For Life is ONLY for people looking to safely and securely grow their money in order to leave a legacy for their family while, importantly, making sure they have the income they need, that they can't outlive.

FOR YOU, WE USE Guaranteed Income For Life structured by our Freedom Protection Plan® as a very safe, secure, conservative investment designed to grow your wealth and with modest returns, give you a helpful monthly paycheck for the rest of your life, and protect your investment as carefully as if it were our own parents'.

Safe, secure, sensible investing. That's what people with good, old-fashioned common sense in or approaching retirement want. People who love our Plan are NOT greedy. They want to be good stewards of their money. NEVER be a burden to their family. ABLE TO CONTINUE supporting church and charities.

And that's what God wants.
God approves of leaving an inheritance. (Proverbs 13:22). He also teaches that it is imperative to provide for one's family. (1 Timothy 5:8). However, all this can be overdone. And misunderstood. "Inheritance" does not mean just cash or property, but the passing along of values, principles, and understanding of how the money came to be and what wise stewardship of it is expected.

Guaranteed Income For Life sets the example for growing your money in a responsible fashion, with tangible benefits you can enjoy now while creating a legacy for your spouse, your kids, the future generations. Sound crazy? It's not.

Is it "normal"? Remember, "normal" investment products are simply the more profitable products Wall Street and financial advisors push on uncertain investors. "Normal" is what investors buy when they don't know what to invest in. "Normal" doesn't mean "better"; It means commonly sold. If you watch financial news like on FOX-Business or CNBC, you'll NEVER see Guaranteed Income For Life discussed, because the truth is, these programs are disguised advertising for Wall Street. Everybody on them pushes stocks.

What's important is investing in products that are right for you, that match your goals and values, NOT that Wall Street prefers to sell. Guaranteed Income For Life is the powerful opportunity you'll discover when you break from "the norm".

CAN YOU INVEST WITH A PLAN THAT INSURES YOUR WAY OF LIVING?

Think about it. You probably have life insurance, to provide for family members IF or WHEN you die. You probably bought it while still relatively young, because you started a family and your children's lives were dependent on your finances.

But you don't have LIVING insurance.
You may have pre-paid long-term care insurance, should you need to move to an assisted living or nursing facility or get in-home nursing care. But that takes care of living under unwanted conditions that hold you captive. Why not insure your LIVING well, while well?

That's what a Guaranteed Income For Life Plan is.

You "paid your dues" 100 times over. You are of the generations that made America great. You worked hard, paid your bills, raised a family. Surely it's worth reviewing all the ways Guaranteed Income For Life can immediately help you…

1. A GUARANTEED PAYCHECK EVERY MONTH FOR THE REST OF YOUR LIFE

The name says it all. Guaranteed Income For Life gives you a monthly paycheck, just like you have been used to receiving your entire career. The size of this monthly payment depends on how much money you put into the Plan. That principal accrues interest.

You get your principal plus earnings when the contract term expires. More importantly, Guaranteed Income For Life gives you an additional income stream to go with your Social Security income benefits, pension, pay-out from selling a business and other investment earnings.

2. IT'S GUARANTEED SAFE

Guaranteed Income For Life is one of the safest investments possible because it guarantees the safety of your principal investment ***regardless of how the market performs***. Each plan is a contract between you and the insurance company backing the Plan. They're committing to (A) return your principal no matter what happens in the market, and (B) they're guaranteeing a return on your investment. No risk, no loss of principal, no matter what happens in the market. Can't say that about your 401k!

The only way it is possible to "lose" money is if you make an early withdrawal that exceeds the agreement's penalty-free withdrawal amount. You will also have to pay taxes on it.

3. YOU GET GUARANTEED RETURNS

With a Guaranteed Income For Life Plan, you get guaranteed returns, on average about 4% to 4.5% per year. ***Even if the market has a down year you get this as your guaranteed paycheck.*** By law, the insurance company backing the Plan must pay you the guaranteed return amount.

4 to 4.5% may seem like a modest amount. But that's much better than interest rates on many CDs, money markets, and bonds. And it's certain. Plus, you still have the potential to earn more in an "up" market. You DO have an "upside." But you have NO "downside".

4. IT CAN BE A GREAT WAY TO SAVE ON TAXES

One affluent, knowledgeable investor using this Plan I know describes Guaranteed Income For Life as "divorcing the IRS". That's because a Guaranteed Income For Life policy lets you accumulate earnings on a tax-deferred basis if you wish, until the Plan expires. You don't have to even worry about taxes until the principal plus earnings are withdrawn.

As a comparison, 401ks are a solid way to build retirement savings. But they have excessive fees, totaling hundreds of dollars PER YEAR for most Americans. Think how much that costs you over 30 or 40 years. Tens of thousands of dollars.

In some cases that could mean years of hard work lost to fees. That's absurd. AND THEN… In the event of your passing, your 401k is going to be taxed 3 times before it passes on to your beneficiaries. 3 times!

Now consider this… if you are no longer working for the company where your 401k was set up, you can roll it into a Guaranteed Income For Life Plan. And when the Plan term ends, you only pay taxes once. That's a serious tax savings.

The truly wealthy (and their full-time accounts) know this. Avoiding taxes—legally, ethically—is very possible. And a Guaranteed Income For Life plan is a great way for anyone to do it.

With your Freedom Protection Plan®, you decide whether you want income now or deferred for later, and you decide when you will take care of the taxes.

5. YOU COULD GET A REALLY BIG BONUS

Guaranteed Income For Life products come with several different penalty-free periods. Most common are 7, 10, and 14 years, after which you're free to withdraw your funds without penalty. Often, when you invest in a 14-year term, you can automatically receive a very big Sign-On Deposit bonus from the participating insurance company. Big as in 20% of your principal paid into your account, guaranteed. That makes you money right out of the gate. And that extra money is going to earn you additional returns over the life of the Plan.

6. NOT PORTFOLIO DIVERSITY — INCOME DIVERSITY

Don't put all your eggs in one basket. Diversify your portfolio. Every investor knows to avoid that. It's a great safety measure that protects you from losing everything all at once. BUT it's still an imperfect protection. If your portfolio is made up of stocks, bonds, ETFs…it is still one basket of market volatility and risk! NO guarantees.

And what about dividend stocks? A popular strategy sold to retirees is owning only dividend-paying stocks. Some pay 4%, some 7%, some even more. The higher the dividend, the less stable the company. It HAS TO offer high dividends to attract capital. BUT the dividend can be reduced or even suspended altogether arbitrarily. Or you get your dividend but the value of your stock falls by a lot more than the dividend. YOU ARE ALWAYS AT RISK!

However, Guaranteed Income For Life from the Freedom Protection Plan® provides you with monthly income that, when paired with your other income streams (Social Security, dividends, pensions, investment earnings) gives you INCOME DIVERSITY. Separate streams of monthly income you can count on to pay expenses, fund your way of living, and live well…all without touching your retirement nest egg.

7. IT REALLY IS GUARANTEED?

We really can say that it's guaranteed. Here's why: The money you invest is attached to a fixed index fund. That means it is not susceptible to the ups and downs of the market. Additionally, your investment is backed by the major insurance company offering the Plan. Even in a down year, they're still obligated to return your invested principal as well as the returns promised on that investment.

For once, guaranteed actually means ***guaranteed***.

In fact, NO failure or disruption of these Plan payments has ever occurred. Savings & Loans have failed, banks have failed, people with deposits exceeding FDIC limits have lost their money, people have waited months to get paid...FDR once declared a "bank holiday" to stop a run on the banks and let no one make withdrawals...corporate pensions get slashed...and, of course, the market itself is very volatile and being dependent on it for your income is nerve-wracking. These Plans EQUAL REAL PEACE OF MIND.

8. GUARANTEED INCOME = GUARANTEED FREEDOM

Having more money coming in regularly always helps, especially in retirement. A Guaranteed Income For Life, Freedom Protection Plan® gives you the freedom to maximize your retirement without having to constantly watch for market ups and downs, pay oppressive taxes, or worry about outliving your money.

Guaranteed Income For Life frees you to truly enjoy your retirement. Indulge in travel. Relax on vacation. Play golf, tennis, or pickleball. It allows you to live generously, donating time to charity, community, or church.

IS GUARANTEED INCOME FOR LIFE FOR YOU?

Yes, it is if you are looking to:

- Invest in a way that protects your principal.
- Accumulate tax-deferred assets
- Have a guaranteed income stream
- Enjoy multiple income streams during retirement
- Guarantee income to a spouse or to a family member with special needs
- Pass on assets to your beneficiaries without delay or cost of probate.
- Reduce taxes on Social Security benefits.
- Never, ever, ever outlive your income.

WHAT TO DO NEXT

GOOD NEWS! This does NOT have to be complicated. We "de-mystify" it. We make it easy for you and your spouse to understand, verify, and feel comfortable with. Safe, secure retirement investing and Guaranteed Income For Life can be fast and done with Wealth Express®.

The Next Step is a no-fee, no obligation meeting with a Wealth Express® Certified Advisor in the privacy of your home. The meeting typically takes from 30 to 90 minutes, about the length of a TV program.

WHAT TO EXPECT FROM YOUR PRIVATE, AT-HOME MEETING

Your Private Meeting with a Wealth Express® Certified Advisor will begin with them asking what you would like your retirement to look like. It's okay if you're not entirely sure. Your Certified Advisor will start to show you what's possible, based on the amount of money you're looking to invest.

They will:

1. Explain how it all works, clearly, understandably

2. Help determine your preferred level of investment

3. Calculate—with real numbers—how much money you can expect to earn over the course of the Plan.

4. Illustrate how these same Plans have performed over the past 10 years.

5. Show you exactly how much your monthly Guaranteed Income For Life paycheck will be.

6. Confirm how much you can withdraw each year with no penalty.

7. Reveal your Initial Deposit Bonus

Rest Assured, Your Privacy Is Respected

We live in an age of "privacy destruction". Every time you try doing anything, even ordering take-out food, you are forced to add an app to your phone, your data is "mined", and God only knows where it goes and who gets it. NOTHING YOU DISCLOSE TO US in discussing the customizing of The Freedom Protection Plan® will leave the room!

Do NOT Worry About "BEING SOLD"

The Freedom Protection Plan® is, ultimately, a PERSONAL decision. We want you to have all the facts and we trust you to make the best decision for you and your family.
There is NO "PRESSURE".

One "Caution"...

At-home meetings are limited. An Advisor has to complete their certification and hold a 2-15 license in your state AND qualify with Wealth Express®. It's not like any "body" off the street can jump in here. Thus there are a very limited number of Certified Advisors in your area. The best way to avoid a long delay in scheduling your Meeting, is to respond as soon as this book makes sense to you.

A BRIEF PERSONAL NOTE

As I said at the beginning, in my 40 years as a pastor, I witnessed a lot of pain and financial embarrassment and shock by retirees and seniors who believed they had a secure retirement—and suddenly had their assets base savaged, and therefore the income they depended on cut in half or worse. This motivated me to make a very serious study of "retirement investing". What I found surprised me—(1) that 90% of all retirees had 50% to 90% of all their savings AT RISK and (2) most had NO guaranteed income as a solid foundation. This led me here. I think of it as my new calling. I am proud of the work we are doing at Wealth Express®. I really pray that you will invite us into your home, to show it all to you. Nothing beats a person-to-person conversation. We live now in an era of isolation-by-internet. I don't like it. I like to shake somebody's hand, look them in the eye, talk with them and, as my father said, "take their measure". Let's do that. And please don't procrastinate.

Tim Whipple

Wealth Express® Ambassador

If you are worried about outliving your money…

If you think you'll never be able to retire…

If you wonder "do I have enough?"…

If you dread having to go back to work during retirement…

If the fate of your savings rests on a volatile stock market…

If you are hesitant to draw on your retirement savings because it's going to get taxed heavily…

If you feel like retirement is
approaching too fast and
you have saved too little…

If you're starting to suspect you
won't have the retirement
you dreamed of…

If "what if's" are keeping
you up at night….

You are NOT alone.

WHO BENEFITS FROM GUARANTEED INCOME FOR LIFE PLANS?

People like these…
people like you.

ACTIVE, LIVELY RETIREES

Why?

Planning ahead…crucial for anyone who cherishes their independence and active lifestyle and who wants to continue doing so in retirement. Whether your plans include taking cruises, dancing, golfing, pickleball, dining out with friends, going to concerts or sporting events, attending church, or treating your grandkids to a movie, you never want to be hampered by second guesses asking, "Can I afford this?"

It's essential to have the financial resources to support your retirement lifestyle.

Inadequate planning can lead to a significant reduction in the quality of life for retirees. Those who fail to prepare may find themselves withdrawing from the activities they once enjoyed, recognizing the decline in their lifestyle as a direct consequence of financial setbacks and poor planning.

Guaranteed Income For Life plans are allowing active seniors to maintain their standard of living and continue enjoying the activities they love until THEY are ready to stop.

SINGLE AND WIDOWED RETIREES

Why?

Many retirees who are single or widowed want to maintain their independence. They DO NOT want to become a burden on their families or friends if they were to face a disability. These individuals are characterized by their pride, dedication, and strong family values. They have spent their lives caring for others and are determined to continue doing so, with no desire to rely on anyone else for their own care.

Guaranteed monthly income—in addition to Social Security—keeps you "in the game."

You DON'T have to stop.
You are able to fully participate in
your pursuits, activities, and dreams.

Safe, secure, stable…Defiant Widows
and Single Seniors are scheduling
Retirement Risk Assessment Meetings
to help them plan a secure
INDEPENDENT future.

PEOPLE WHO TAKE THEIR FINANCES AND RETIREMENT SERIOUSLY AND TAKE RESPONSIBILITY FOR IT.

Why?

They read up on the world, watch the markets, read the papers, research. They stay informed. They know what's going on, enough to know it's best to stay away from Wall Street.

Guaranteed Income For Life clients are exceptionally proactive when it comes to managing their retirement finances.

Their desire to avoid the unpredictability of Wall Street and conventional financial strategies is precisely why they choose to work with Wealth Express®.

These clients are committed to doing everything possible to protect their current lifestyle throughout retirement. They understand the importance of diversifying their income, securing a consistent monthly retirement paycheck, and safeguarding their finances from excessive government taxation.

THE RETIRED OR SOON-TO-BE RETIREES WITH A NEED FOR INCOME FROM THEIR LIFE'S SAVINGS WITHOUT UNDUE RISK

Why?

They DO have good reason to worry.
They DO need to achieve the best possible income from their assets with ZERO RISK. Because they are past the age where they can recover from a big loss.

The watching, the worrying…the stress of market ups and downs. It gets old. It takes a toll.
And your money is ALWAYS at risk.

Loss of principal is NOT an option.

The Cautiously Retired rely on Guaranteed Income For Life precisely because it eliminates the risk. It zaps the worry. It builds CERTAINTY.

WOMEN RESPONSIBLE FOR THEIR OWN FINANCES OR WHO MAY BECOME RESPONSIBLE FOR THEIR OWN FINANCES.

Why?

Even as women's incomes have grown, research shows that many women still tend to delegate financial decisions to their husbands. This often leaves them unprepared to take charge in situations like a spouse's disability or death.

Women, newly widowed, thrust into a caretaking role… are often investing in Guaranteed Income For Life plans because they can "set it and forget it."

PEOPLE WITH "TAX BOMBS"

Why?

You have "done the right things". Maximized contributions to IRA, 401k, Keough, SEP, other retirement accounts and plans. You've invested in tax-deferred vehicles…perhaps hold appreciated real estate…and now as you reach retirement, your time to savor life, you go to cash in on investments only to detonate a tax bomb you never expected.

Some of your gains might face taxation at income rates, not capital gains rates. There are always new income and capital gains tax increases in the works. And no…

The government does NOT care that you already paid taxes on the original income nor that you saved and invested only what they let you keep after taxes. They want to tax you again!

People with tax deferred investments and retirement accounts who do not want to be exposed to ticking tax bombs turn to Guaranteed Income For Life accounts. Because they provide a perfectly legal and simple way to re-defer these taxes or even outfox them altogether.

PEOPLE WHO WANT TO ENJOY THEIR RETIREMENT ARE A PERFECT FIT FOR WEALTH EXPRESS®

Why?

It's called "retirement" for a reason. You want to travel, get to the golf course often, pursue hobbies you've waited decades to indulge, spend time with family and friends WITHOUT WORRY. You want to sleep well at night. You DON'T want to hunch over your desk for hours, squinting and studying dozens of financial documents, worrying daily about investment decisions.

Two things can and will undermine the freedom and financial peace of mind you seek. One, "scattered financial pieces"; money invested here, there, everywhere. Just keeping up with it all is stressful. Two, worry over insufficient lifetime income for husband and wife or for a surviving spouse. Our clients feel at ease, availed of their worries.

When a client puts their money in a Guaranteed Income For life plan…the worrying can STOP.

CALL: (833) 600-2832
To schedule your meeting with a
Wealth Express® Certified Advisor now.
CODE: WSA115

WHY YOU CAN'T RELY ON GOVERNMENT

Presidential candidate for a time, Gov. Nikki Haley flatly stated that **Social Security would be BROKE AND BANKRUPT within 10 years and that "adjustments" to it had to be made NOW**.

At the city and state level, many services and benefits for seniors and others are being compromised – due to the costs of caring for illegal migrants!

Muni-bonds, ie. municipal, are rendered INSECURE AND UNSAFE by this. Towns and cities have gone bankrupt and many will in coming years.

The "affluent" retiree, with a paid-for home, with money in 401K and IRA accounts or pension plans, is A TARGET of tax "reform" and Social Security "reform."

HERE IS WHAT YOU ARE UP AGAINST:

- Wall Street Uncertainty and Thievery
- Deliberately Confusing Plans and Products
- A Government Desperate For Cash

We owe $35 Trillion.
We borrow more every day,
reaching unsustainable levels.

What will they do???

CHANGE MEDICARE?

TAX SOCIAL SECURITY BENEFITS?

IMPOSE NEW "WEALTH" TAXES?

We've suffered runaway inflation. Overall, up 17% total since President Biden took office. But some things are worse, like eggs, meat, car and home insurance. This basically takes 17%, 22%, 24% of your saved dollars away.

What if this continues? Or slows, but re-starts?

What has inflation, sky-high interest rates, college costs….done to your sons and daughters and grandchildren? Kept them from getting their first home? Kept them from college? Put them deep in debt?

BROUGHT THEM TO YOUR DOORSTEP, FOR MORE FINANCIAL HELP?

There is no cure for all of it – inflation, interest rates, likely changes to Social Security, Wall Street risks.

BUT…

...HERE IS WHAT IS POSSIBLE:

- Lock in income you can't outlive, guaranteed for life

    YES! ...for consistent income AFTER you stop working, arriving every month right on time

- Get a 4% to 7% yield, SAFELY. With SAFETY FIRST!

    YES! ...with zero risk to your principal. The money you worked hard to earn, to save

- Get a monthly paycheck

    YES! ...so you never have "more month than money", never limit your living

- Have this income untouchable by the government

    YES! ...It is yours. Secured vault-like in a plan they cannot touch, unlike banks and qualified retirement accounts.

- Have this income guaranteed and protected and safe from lawsuits

    YES! ... This money is PRIVATE from all peepers, including the IRS, creditors, ANYONE.

CALL: (833) 600-2832

To schedule your meeting with a
Wealth Express® Certified Advisor now.
CODE: WSA116

SOCIAL SECURITY

WARNING:

Social Security, Medicare, And Other Gov't Benefit Programs Are NOT Guaranteed. They Are NOT "LOCKED IN". They CAN Be Changed. At Any Moment.

EVERY DAY, 10,000 MORE BOOMERS TURN 65…..

That's 10,000 more Americans qualifying for payments from Social Security, health care costs paid by Medicare, services from their states and cities.

EVERY DAY, BIDEN HAS WELCOMED THOUSANDS OF NEW, ILLEGAL MIGRANTS INTO AMERICA…… NINE-MILLION+ since he took office….scattered throughout the country…..demanding cities and towns provide shelter, housing, meals, health care, K-12 school, and more…..adding to already dangerous street crime, increasing the load on de-funded and shrunken police. Cities are at breaking points.

There may be a huge federal bail-out coming.

But there HAS TO BE a coming Day of Reckoning. We already have trouble selling our debt. There is more and more talk of China replacing our dollar with their yen as the world's reserve currency. Remember the 2008 crisis? And raising our debt ceiling has become a bi-annual game of partisan "chicken", with shutting down government services at risk.

CAN YOU COUNT ON THIS 'SYSTEM' FOR YOUR RETIREMENT SECURITY?

Consider…

A Guaranteed Income For Life plan can change retirement income calculations **to your advantage**.

Having a floor beneath you that CAN'T fall…
simply makes sense.

GARY + JUDY

Gary and Judy Thompson were the picture of middle-class America. A couple who worked hard, lived within their means, and raised their children with love and discipline. Gary spent his entire career as a plumber, a job that was physically demanding but provided a solid income. Judy dedicated her life to nursing, but not in a typical hospital setting. She worked at the elementary school run by their church. Modest pay, but it offered immense personal satisfaction.

The Thompsons never lived extravagantly, but they were comfortable. Their humble home was paid off by the time their children, Pete and Sadie, went to college. They didn't take lavish vacations, but they cherished their annual trips to the beach, where they'd spend a week relaxing by the shore, enjoying the simple pleasures of sun, sand, and family. They were the kind of couple who believed in giving back to their community, donating regularly to their church and volunteering whenever they could.

From the early days of their marriage, Gary and Judy understood the importance of saving for retirement. They weren't financial experts, but they knew they couldn't rely solely on Social Security. So, they did what they thought was best: they opened an IRA, contributed to Gary's 401(k) when his employer offered it, and even dabbled in the stock market, purchasing shares of well-known companies. They didn't have a formal financial plan, but they trusted that their steady saving would be enough to carry them through their golden years.

As the years passed, their children grew up and started families of their own. Pete became an engineer, while Sadie followed in her mother's footsteps and became a nurse. Gary and Judy were proud of their children and looked forward to spending their retirement years spoiling their grandchildren, traveling a bit, relaxing—finally—after decades of hard work.

When Gary turned 65, he decided it was time to retire. He'd put in more than 40 years as a plumber, and the wear and tear to his body was catching up. Judy, a few years younger, decided to retire as well, eager to enjoy their time together. They paid their dues and saved carefully, and believed they had enough to maintain their lifestyle—*why not enjoy it?*

They had no problem settling into retirement.
It felt GOOD. Until…

Gary and Judy quickly realized that things weren't as simple, or secure, as they had hoped. Inflation kept creeping up. Their cost of living increased dramatically. Groceries, utilities, healthcare—*how can they charge these kind of prices!?* Everything became more expensive, more than they planned for. Even simple pleasures like taking the grandkids to McDonald's had doubled in price. What used to be a $20 outing now cost over $40.

This did not sit well with Gary. He had always prided himself on being a good provider. But now…what to do? He couldn't stop worrying about their finances. Watching the stock market fluctuate wildly really took a number on his nerves, to where he wasn't feeling so good. Judy, seeing her husband's distress, felt compelled to help. She returned to work at the school, but it had never been a lot of money. Worse, she didn't love the idea of taking money from the very church she wished she could still donate to.

Gary, too, tried to return to work. But at 66, well… plumbing was no longer a sustainable option. The physical demands of the job were too much for his aging body, and when he threw out his back trying to fix a leaky pipe, he knew it was time to hang up his tools for good. With limited skills outside of plumbing, the only job Gary could find was bagging groceries at the local market store. Honest work indeed, and he took pride in doing it well, but he found it difficult not to be bitter.

What happened to the retirement we saved for, filled with leisure, travel, relaxing with Judy?

After being on his feet for hours each day, nights became a time of recovery, not relaxation.

> Gary and Judy were both exhausted,
> *wondering WHAT HAPPENED??*

As they sat together one evening, Gary expressed his regrets. "I thought we did everything right," he said quietly. "We saved, we invested, but it just wasn't enough." Judy squeezed his hand, sharing his sentiments. "We just didn't know how to plan for this."

The truth was, Gary and Judy had planned but they did not plan strategically.

They hadn't considered how or how much inflation, market volatility, and healthcare costs would impact their retirement. They hadn't explored options like a Guaranteed Income for Life plan, which could have provided them with a steady monthly income, reducing their reliance on the unpredictable stock market and allowing them to delay taking Social Security. This decision alone, waiting to claim Social Security, could have added a great deal of their retirement income, money they now desperately needed.

With the right guidance, Gary and Judy would have enjoyed the retirement instead of enduring regrets. they always dreamed of—one filled with travel, time with family, and the peace of mind that comes from financial security.

Planning, Not Just Saving

Dinner with friends (and *comfortable* retirees) brought Guaranteed Income For Life plans to Gary and Judy's attention. They were intrigued, hopeful, wasted no time. *They learned how* they could put their savings to better use. *They learned how* moving the money over <u>would</u> protect it, **secure and safe, yet available**—they WOULD be able to get cash each month for the rest of their lives. *They learned how* they could minimize, perhaps eliminate, some taxes.

So that's what they did. They invested in Guaranteed Income For Life. They activated their "retirement paycheck". They SAVED their retirement.

And that's not all.

Gary and Judy made a point to share the retirement-saving knowledge they learned with their grown children. That way, when it was time for Peter and Sadie to get serious about retirement, they would be prepared, they would have a plan.

Is Your Spouse Secretly Worried….Sometimes Tense or Irritable…about Money & Finances?

DO YOU TAKE THIS PERSONALLY?

Think: why am I being questioned? Well, it's important to understand that your partner may not share the same knowledge or confidence that you have about money matters. An uncertain future in retirement, with paychecks stopped, Social Security and Medicare eyed by a cash-strapped government, inflation, an erratic stock market, worries about health and medical needs…..the news on radio, TV, in the newspaper….talk with friends….. can all make your spouse anxious, and unconsciously, take it out on you.

(continued...)

YOU CAN STOP THIS ANXIETY.

**Simple. Easy. Fast.
DONE.**

Imagine the relief your spouse will feel.

The first step is scheduling your FREE of cost or obligation Retirement Risk Assessment Meeting.

CALL: (833) 600-2832
To schedule your meeting with a
Wealth Express® Certified Advisor now.
CODE: WSA135

WHY ARE WE NAMED
"WEALTH EXPRESS®"?

Because we SIMPLIFY the complicated, "PLAIN ENGLISH" the explanation, and make it EASY to CONFIDENTLY make decisive financial decisions without worry or confusion over having done the right thing – then "SET IT & FORGET IT".

Your Personal Freedom Protection Plan is a machine that smartly, safely runs itself. You can ignore the markets, market volatility, the financial news, etc. during a day on the golf course or a 10-day Caribbean cruise or a month traveling Europe and never worry….but if you want to, you can still share in market gains.

This is:
PROTECTED FREEDOM
= REAL WEALTH.

Whether we do business together or not, whether we have the privilege of serving you or not…

Wealth Express® is <u>committed</u> to doing everything we can to help relieve the URGENT AND GROWING national retirement crisis.

And you WILL benefit from your Retirement Risk Assessment Meeting.

CALL: (833) 600-2832

To schedule your meeting with a Wealth Express® Certified Advisor now.
CODE: WSA117

I'LL BET

I'll bet you've worked hard,
played by the rules, made sacrifices
for your family, been a good neighbor,
and I'll bet you love your wife.

I'll bet you stand for our anthem,
kneel to pray and SINCERELY
thank veterans for their service.

YOU are the exact person
Wealth Express® was created to help.

We love seeing people like you have
LIFE-CHANGING EXPERIENCES after
getting a rock-solid foundation laid and
levelled for enduring financial security.

3 THINGS YOU NEED TO KNOW…

First…
Neither Washington nor Wall Street contains friends or allies truly concerned that you'll have the secure retirement you've earned a right to, a dozen times over.

Second…
Getting a good income from your life's savings, making sure you'll have access to top medical care without being forced into bankruptcy, getting it, guarding against 'tax time bombs' embedded in your retirement accounts, etc – are complicated. Tackling all of this alone, frankly, just isn't a smart thing to do.

Third…
You can be much more secure with a trustworthy, trusted Wealth Express® Certified Advisor collaborating with you on a personalized plan and watching out for you in this very uncertain and volatile economy.

I know you know these things.

FOUNDATION FIRST

It's hard to find a building standing that didn't have its foundation built first. Recently, I had a back-up generator installed at my house – the kind you see advertised on TV. They didn't just drop the generator anywhere, on uneven ground. They picked the best place then laid a flat, solid, weather-proof foundation for it.

We believe that Guaranteed Income For Life should be your financial foundation.

MARGARET

"I never imagined my life would take the turn it did when I lost my dear husband, Darryl, two years ago."

He was my rock, my partner, and the love of my life. For over 40 years, we shared everything—our home, our children, our dreams—but when it came to finances, Darryl always took the lead. It wasn't that I couldn't handle the numbers; it's just that we fell into a rhythm that worked for us. He managed the bills, the investments, and the savings, while I focused on raising our family and making our house a home. It was a partnership that worked perfectly, until the day he was no longer here.

Darryl's passing was sudden. The shock of losing him was profound, and in the midst of my grief, I was faced with the task of taking over our finances. I was intimidated and completely overwhelmed. For the first time in my life, I had to figure out how to manage everything on my own. I can't tell you how much sleep I lost over it. Those horrible evenings staring at bills spread across the kitchen table, feeling LOST. I just wanted Darryl to take care of it.

Turns out, he did.

Yes, I still had to get up to speed and take care of the monthly bills, some basic money management. But when it came to having enough money, Darryl, my Mr. Meticulous, made sure I would always be taken care of.

He had always told me, "Don't worry about the future, Margaret. We have a plan in place." At the time, I didn't pay much attention to the details; I trusted him completely. It wasn't until he passed that I discovered the full extent of his careful planning.

Darryl had invested in a Guaranteed Income For Life plan, something he had researched and believed in deeply. At a minimum, this plan provides me with steady money, every month, right there in the mailbox. It's money I can and do rely on. Along with my Social Security, which was reduced after Darryl's death, this extra monthly money keeps me comfortable. Darryl would never want me to worry about money, and I don't. I'm so grateful.

I play Mahjong with a group of wonderful ladies at the community center. We meet every Tuesday afternoon, and the hours we spend together are filled with laughter, friendly competition, and camaraderie. It's a small pleasure, but one that I cherish deeply. I also find solace in painting and gardening—two hobbies that allow me to express myself and feel connected to the beauty of the world around me. And when I need a change of scenery, I love visiting museums, losing myself in art and history.

I can do this thanks to Darryl and "his plan."

Perhaps the greatest joy of all is the ability to visit my children and grandchildren regularly. They're spread across the country—my son in California, my daughter in New York—and thanks to the financial security Darryl provided, I can afford to fly out to see them as often as I like. Being with my grandchildren, watching them grow, and being an active part of their lives is a blessing beyond measure. The thought of not being able to see them often, simply because I couldn't afford the travel, is heartbreaking.

I know it would have broken Darryl's heart too, and I'm thankful every day that he made sure I wouldn't have to face that reality.

Every day, I miss Darryl. He was a good man, a loving husband, and such a devoted father. Losing him has been the hardest thing I've ever gone through, and there are days when the grief feels just as fresh as it did the day he passed. But I take comfort in knowing that he continues to care for me even after he's gone. In his final moments, I asked Darryl, "Do you have any unfinished business?" He said, "No, I'm ready to go. I am at peace."

Now, I know why.

Darryl knew his careful planning and getting the Plan would allow me to move forward, to find a new normal, and to continue living a life that honors the love and partnership we shared. I know he would be pleased to see that I'm doing well, that I'm taking care of myself, and that I'm still finding joy in life, even without him by my side.

Darryl's gift has made all the difference. I am forever grateful.

CALL: (833) 600-2832
To schedule your meeting with a
Wealth Express® Certified Advisor now.
CODE: WSA118

IS YOUR RETIREMENT INSURED?

You know insurance…
To cover your car, your house, your home.

You know of life insurance…
In the event of your passing.

**You've likely heard of, perhaps own,
Final Expense aka burial insurance…**

For funeral costs that must be paid in advance (before the life insurance money arrives)…to spare your grieving family.

But do you have Retirement Insurance?
That protects your money from drying up…
That eases reliance on Social Security…
That provides "cash comfort" when your
working days are done.

That's what a Guaranteed Income For Life Plan IS.

Your retirement's cash contingency plan.

CALL: (833) 600-2832
To schedule your meeting with a
Wealth Express® Certified Advisor now.
CODE: WSA119

DID YOU KNOW?...

Sleep problems are now
the #1 complaint of
worried boomers and seniors.

Nearly 1 in 2 older adults
say their biggest financial fear
is not having enough money
saved for retirement.

Those most worried are
between 55 and 64.

A better plan = better sleep.

HOW WOULD YOU LIKE A RETIREMENT INCOME "PAY RAISE"?

IF YOU PURCHASED/INVESTED IN ANY ANNUITIES PRE-2021, A LOT HAS CHANGED.......

I'm an annuities owner for many sensible reasons. But I'm also an annuities professional, an analyst, constantly reviewing the entire annuities marketplace. It really is a "jungle out there". I'm writing because a lot has changed with annuities since 2021 and **you may, UNKNOWINGLY, be "caged" in annuities robbing you of available, maximum gains or income**. Or leaving you exposed to coming tax bombs. One way or another, poorly serving you.

A retirement income PAY RAISE may be waiting for you, right now! Could you use an extra $250, $500, $2,000 a month? Why not claim it?

When you have worked hard, played by the rules, raised a family, saved responsibly and come to semi-retirement or retirement, **it's time for your money to work for you, after years of you working for money. That money must not be allowed to be lazy**! It can't be permitted to rob you of the maximum income you deserve. It should never surprise you with tax costs you didn't see coming.

WHAT YOU MAY NOT KNOW & PROBABLY HAVEN'T BEEN TOLD

1: Many annuities can be exited without surrender charges or penalties

2: TAX-FREE EXCHANGES, just like with real estate, can be done with most annuities – so you CAN move your money

3: Many pre-2021 annuities have you locked in… imprisoned…with lower, poorer interest, income or gains than current markets offer and you CAN move to better, higher yields. There is probably no need for you to settle for less income or gains than are available to you!

4: Many pre-2021 have undisclosed or misunderstood layered fees inside, reducing your income invisibly and this CAN be fixed

5: Many people are invested in annuities without a fully organized, carefully thought through plan for the "mix" of income gains, tax delay, estate planning, and they own a "grab bag" of different annuities (and insurance policies) bought at different times, placed with different companies…..and they could be much better served by the same amount of invested money

6: Many pre-2021 annuities have "secret time bombs" ticking away inside them, guaranteed to explode at some time & many can be "de-fused" (but you can easily be "too late")

7: Your annuity's safety is only as good as the issuing company's financial stability. Many issuers are over-invested in commercial real estate, regional banks, troubled geographic areas and may well be "riskier" than you know

A GUARANTEED INCOME FOR LIFE PLAN CAN HELP

1: These plans are a smart choice for smart annuity investors!

2: There are options for handling the inevitable taxes – you can **legally have tax-free retirement income for life** if that is important to you

3: It can allow you to share in market gains but avoid losses. If you have NOT participated in market gains in the past 5 years, you've missed out on tens of thousands of dollars or more that could have added to the total value of your annuities. But you haven't missed out on all the inflation, have you? Can you really afford "lazy money"?????

4: Today's interest rates are at record highs – NOW is the time to rearrange the money you have in annuities. There may never be this opportune time again in your entire lifetime!

5: Hidden tax bombs in pre-2021 annuities can still be de-fused!

6: Guaranteed Income For Life plans do not necessarily lock you in; there's a period when they act like bank CD's; then a time when you can select lifetime income options OR withdraw your money and gains

IMPORTANT: Your annuity issuers are **<u>NOT REQUIRED</u>** by law to inform you of changes in available, alternative annuities or other financial products released since 2021.

YOUR FREE, NO-FEE, NO-OBLIGATION RETIREMENT RISK ASSESSMENT MEETING CAN GIVE YOU A SECOND OPINION EXAM OF YOUR ANNUITIESAND OTHER INVESTMENTS BY A WEALTH EXPRESS® CERTIFIED ADVISOR

This is done with you….in a private meeting…. at your convenience….relaxed and stress-free. It's a "judgment-free zone". with no criticism of any of your investing up until now. We know that decisions that were perfectly sensible 2 or 3 or 5 or 7 years ago may look very differently now – that's a reason we do this Exam. Everything is completely confidential. If you are perfectly invested as-is, we will most certainly reassure you of that. If, however, there are either hidden hazards or future surprise costs, unnecessary "locks", or better opportunities for you to enjoy a higher income, we will show you those facts and opinions.

If you can easily, safely claim a retirement income pay raise, why miss out?

WHY YOU SHOULD ACT RIGHT NOW - NOT LATER, WHEN YOU GET AROUND TO IT

Sorry, but this is NOT like cleaning out the garage or attic! – something that can be left 'til whenever without any harm.

You may ALREADY be missing out
on higher, better interest rates, income or gains NOT provided by your pre-2021 annuities. Every day "cheats you" out of available income and benefits – and you don't even know what you're losing! Every day matters.

RAGING, SKYROCKETED COSTS OF LIVING have you paying 30% to 50% more than just 3 years ago for your lifestyle needs, from groceries to car maintenance and insurance to home repairs to dining out. While the rate of increase of inflation may moderate, these prices increases aren't going to magically disappear.

Has your income from your investments kept pace? Can it? If your net spending power DECREASES each year, are you walking downhill toward a cliff?

You may have dangerous, hidden tax bombs or other budding costs inside your pre-2021 annuities that, if addressed soon enough, can be de-fused.
A day may decide your gain or pain.

There may never be a more opportune time to make changes.

CALL: (833) 600-2832
To schedule your meeting with a
Wealth Express® Certified Advisor now.
CODE: WSA120

THE BENEFITS OF DELAYING SOCIAL SECURITY BENEFITS

We all know…

Social Security is a crucial component of retirement planning for most Americans. Stable, predictable income for when your working days are done.

Most people DON'T know…

One of the most important decisions you'll make regarding Social Security is WHEN to start claiming your benefits. **The age at which you begin taking Social Security can significantly impact the total amount of income benefits you receive over the course of your retirement.** This decision has long-term financial implications that should be carefully considered.

The Social Security Administration (SSA) designates a specific age as your "Full Retirement Age" (FRA). This age is determined by your birth year. For those born between 1943 and 1954, the FRA is 66. For individuals born in 1960 or later, the FRA is 67.

If you start claiming Social Security at your FRA, you'll receive 100% of your entitled benefit.

However…

You do have the option to start receiving Social Security as early as age 62. While this might seem appealing, especially if you retire early, there's a catch: **taking benefits before your FRA results in a PERMANENT reduction in your monthly benefit amount**.

The decision of when to claim Social Security is highly personal and depends on various factors, including your financial situation, health, and retirement goals. However, the benefit of delaying your benefits is clear.

You WILL receive substantially more money if you wait.

There is no better way to avoid short-changing your Social Security benefits than with a Guaranteed Income For Life plan that provides a retirement paycheck each and every month.

It takes the burden off your Social Security income.

RONALD & CHESTER –
A TALE OF TWO RETIREMENTS

In the small, close-knit town of Auburn, Indiana, two boys named Ronald and Chester grew up as the best of friends. From elementary school through high school, they were inseparable; their childhood filled with shared adventures, laughter, and dreams of the future. Auburn was the kind of place where everyone knew each other, and where kids could roam freely, riding their bikes down quiet streets, trading baseball cards at the local park, and eventually, awkwardly navigating the world of dating as they grew older.

When it came time for college, Ronald and Chester once again found themselves walking the same path. They both attended the same state university, where they roomed together and pursued degrees in business. Both young men were bright and hardworking.

But as they prepared to enter the workforce, their paths began to diverge in subtle, yet significant ways.

RONALD:
THE HIGH-FLYING VICE PRESIDENT

Ronald was charismatic, confident with had a natural flair for leadership. These qualities served him well during job interviews, and after graduation, he quickly landed a management position at a prominent manufacturing company in Auburn. Ronald's quick rise through the ranks was nothing short of impressive. He had a knack for making the right connections, and his superiors took notice.

Within a few years, he was promoted to Vice President, a position that brought with it a substantial salary, perks, and prestige.

Life was good for Ronald. He married a wonderful woman, and together they had two children. They moved into a spacious home in an upscale neighborhood, drove luxury cars, took lavish vacations. Ronald became accustomed to the finer things, and he wasn't shy about spending his money.

However, Ronald's spending habits didn't leave much room for saving. He contributed to his 401(k) and had some investments in the stock market, but these were afterthoughts rather than priorities. Retirement seemed like a distant concern, something to worry about later. As long as he was earning a good salary, there would always be enough money.

CHESTER: THE STEADY FOREMAN

Chester, on the other hand, was more reserved and pragmatic. He didn't have Ronald's flair for management, and although he was just as intelligent and capable, he didn't interview as well. When he applied for jobs after graduation, he landed a position as a foreman at the same manufacturing company where Ronald worked. Chester's role was different; he worked on the factory floor, managing the day-to-day operations and ensuring that everything ran smoothly.

While Chester didn't have the same level of income as Ronald, he made a decent living. He married Rita, a kind and supportive woman, and together they had two children, much like Ronald's family. However, Chester's approach to money was very different than his friend's. He knew that his salary, while sufficient, required careful management. A modest home, reliable car, no unnecessary luxuries.

Chester contributed as much as he could to his 401(k) and opened a Roth IRA. Chester also took the time to educate himself about personal finance. His goal was simple: to ensure that he and his family would be financially secure, no matter what life threw at them.

THE DIVERGING PATHS: RETIREMENT APPROACHES

As the years passed, Ronald and Chester continued to excel in their respective careers. Ronald enjoyed the perks of his high-paying job, while Chester found satisfaction in the stability and predictability of his work. Both men raised their children, who eventually went off to college and started families of their own. Life moved forward, and before they knew it, retirement was on the horizon.

Ronald, now in his late 50s, began to think seriously about retirement for the first time. He began to review his financial situation, he realized that his savings were not as robust as he had hoped. He had some money in his 401(k) and a few investments, but he had never prioritized saving. His portfolio had also taken a hit during a market downturn, and the recovery was slower than he anticipated.

When Ronald retired at 65, he found himself dipping into savings much sooner than planned. His Social Security benefits, while helpful, had no hope of sustaining the lifestyle he and his wife had grown accustomed to. As his savings dwindled, the financial strain began to take a toll on his marriage. Ronald and his wife found themselves arguing more frequently, the stress of their financial situation weighing heavily on both of them.

Meanwhile, Chester and Rita had quietly, carefully prepared for retirement for decades, building a solid financial foundation. By the time they were ready to retire, they were in position to live off of just his Guaranteed Income For Life plan and modest earnings from other investments. Chester and Rita deliberately delayed claiming his Social Security benefits until he reached 70.

This strategy paid off handsomely, providing them with a comfortable income that exceeded their needs.

THE RETIREMENT YEARS: A TALE OF TWO FUTURES

Ronald's financial troubles began to impact his marriage. The strain of making ends meet led to frequent arguments with his wife, and the couple found themselves drifting apart. The retirement Ronald had envisioned—a time of relaxation, travel, and enjoyment—was slipping away, replaced by a daily struggle to keep their heads above water.

Chester and Rita thrived in retirement. Their careful planning made retirement everything they had hoped for. He spent his days refurbishing classic cars and expanding his collection of valuable baseball cards. He and Rita traveled frequently, visited the children and grandchildren, and always arrived with gifts. They were truly, to their core, happy.

Ronald's story proves why millions of Americans—especially high earners enjoying their money as they earn it—are staring down an uncertain, unsettling retirement reality. Chester's story proves our guiding principal:

You don't need to be rich to retire; you just need a plan.

YOUR SIX IMPORTANT QUESTIONS WILL BE ANSWERED AT YOUR FREE IN-HOME MEETING WITH A WEALTH EXPRESS® CERTIFIED ADVISOR

1. Are my Social Security and Medicare benefits guaranteed?

2. Which should be more important to you, based on your financial situation and your retirement goals?

3. Do I have enough GUARANTEED lifetime income for my needs?

4. Do I have guaranteed income SAFE from lawsuits, medical bills, medical bankruptcy, or other "disasters"?

5. How can safe, secure retirement income, guaranteed, be made simple and easy.

6. Is there a gap in my financial plan to consider?

WOULD YOU RATHER…

1. …Spend your retirement traveling the world, visiting new places, and experiencing different cultures OR stay home because you can't afford to travel beyond your own town?

2. …Enjoy your retirement days pursuing hobbies you love, like golfing, painting, or gardening OR work a part-time job in your 70s just to pay the bills?

3. …Live in a comfortable, paid-off home with the freedom to enjoy your golden years OR worry about paying rent or a mortgage each month because your savings ran out?

4. …Have the financial security to spoil your grandchildren with gifts and fun outings OR feel the stress of not being able to contribute to their birthdays or holidays?

5. …Enjoy a peaceful retirement without financial stress, knowing your bills are covered OR constantly argue with your spouse about money and how to make ends meet?

6. …Have the freedom to dine out at your favorite restaurants whenever you wish OR be forced to cook every meal at home because eating out is too expensive?

7. …Have the peace of mind to handle unexpected expenses, like medical bills or home repairs OR face the anxiety of wondering how you'll pay for emergencies as they arise?

8. …Improvise a risk-filled retirement OR wouldn't you rather let us help you eliminate "money stress" so can live the American dream you have earned?

CALL: (833) 600-2832

To schedule your meeting with a
Wealth Express® Certified Advisor now.
CODE: WSA121

Made in the USA
Columbia, SC
04 November 2024